THE SAME SEA IN US ALL

JAAN KAPLINSKI was born in Tartu, Estonia, in 1941. His mother was Estonian, and his father, who disappeared into a Stalinist labour camp while the poet was still a child, was Polish. Kaplinski studied Romance languages and structural and mathematical linguistics at Tartu State University and has since been a student of anthropology, especially of the works of Paul Radin, Claude Levi-Strauss, and the linguist Benjamin Whorf. He has translated from the Spanish, French, English, Polish and Chinese, and provided the literal translations for this collection. He is also a serious student of Mahayana Buddhism, and of the philosophies of India, China, Japan, and Korea. Although his native language of Estonian has been officially replaced by Russian, his poetry has gained him a reputation as one of Eastern Europe's most gifted poets. In addition, he is an essayist and a professor with several books published in his homeland. He lives in Tartu with his wife and son, and teaches at the State University there. A second collection of Kaplinski's work, *The Wandering Border*, will be published by Harvill Paperbacks in due course.

Sam Hamill is co-publisher with Tree Swenson at Copper Canyon Press, Washington, USA. He is the author of seven collections of poetry, including *Fatal Pleasure* (1987), and has translated several volumes of poetry from the Chinese, as well as selected poems of Catullus from the Latin.

By the same author

THE WANDERING BORDER

Jaan Kaplinski

THE SAME SEA
IN US ALL

Translated from the Estonian by
the Author and Sam Hamill

COLLINS HARVILL
8 Grafton Street, London W1
1990

COLLINS HARVILL
William Collins Sons & Co. Ltd
London · Glasgow · Sydney · Auckland
Toronto · Johannesburg

BRITISH LIBRARY CATALOGUING IN PUBLICATION DATA

Kaplinski, Jaan, *1941–*
The same sea in us all.
I. Title   II. Hamill, Sam
894'.54512

ISBN 0-00-271091-9

Grateful acknowledgement is made to the editors of the following
publications in which some of these poems first appeared: *Willow
Springs*; *New Directions Annual*; *Chariton Review*; *Alcatraz*; *North-
west Review*; *Prism*; *Another Chicago Magazine*; *Crab Creek Review*;
Poetry Now; *Paris Review*.

First published in the USA by Breitenbush Books 1985
First published in Great Britain by Collins Harvill 1990

© Jaan Kaplinski and Sam Hamill 1985

Printed and bound in Great Britain by
Hartnolls Limited, Bodmin, Cornwall

CONTENTS

PART THREE

An asterisk (*) indicates a Note on the Poem.

Introduction

ESTONIA is a tiny country bordering the east coast of the Gulf of Finland. It is the westernmost representative of non-western mentality, its language being Finno-Ugric, most closely related to Finnish. Its citizens have endured over eight hundred years of imposed government. Following the fall of Czarist Russia in 1917, Estonia established its independence and was admitted to the League of Nations in 1921. But Estonian national integrity fell victim to the Russo-German Non-Aggression Pact of 1940, and Russia established military bases there immediately. Germany occupied the country from 1941 to 1944, but with the collapse of the Third Reich, Estonia was returned to the hands of Stalinist Russia.

Jaan Kaplinski was born in Tartu, Estonia, in 1941, the son of a Polish father and Estonian mother. His father disappeared into Stalin's labor camps while Kaplinski was still a small child. He studied Romance languages and structural and mathematical linguistics at Tartu State University, and has since been a student of anthropology, especially of the works of Paul Radin, Claude Levi-Strauss, and the linguist Benjamin Whorf. Among his early works are translations from the Spanish, French, English, and Polish.

Kaplinski is a serious student of Mahayana Buddhism as well, and of the philosophies of India, China, Japan, and Korea. He credits as a major source of his creative expression the deep suffering of the world, the grief of remembrance, the killing of animals, the fate of Third World nations, and the destruction of wilderness. He often quotes the Hebrew master who observed that Paradise must exist because the world in which we live is most certainly Hell.

But Kaplinski is not a grim or hopeless poet. Even though his life offers plenty of reasons to despair (the loss of his father at a tender age, the bloodshed and carnage and destruction of World War Two, the fact that he is the father of a severely handicapped child), Kaplinski's early poems suggest that the world suffers mostly from the forces of irrationality; and while brutality may be endured, the irrational is more devastating. His more recent poems move away from the Western concept of duality, and discover the healing properties of poetic transcendence, a power which moves, in Kaplinski's words, "like waves – the highs and lows shifting, interchanging... and somehow connecting to the mytho-poetical archetype, wiping away what has been, bringing into focus a holy beginning." Through his Buddhist training, Kaplinski has moved away from the dualistic vision and into a "middle way" based upon balance and self-discipline, a practice that permits a freedom concerned not with achieving residence in some distant Paradise, but rather in realization of the Paradise that is within.

"A man's Paradise," Ezra Pound said, paraphrasing Kung-fu Tze, "is his own good nature." Kaplinski's poems often are incantations echoing the shamanic tradition of primitive Uralic-Altaic peoples, but which include the poet's interest in early Marx and the history of religions. In an essay on Utopian ethics and prejudice, he relates Marxism to other ideologies of discontent including early Christian philosophy. His poems invite us to embrace our human-ness, for Marx, like the Gnostics and other Christian-Taoist-Buddhist-primitive metaphysicians, believed that our unhappiness and dissatisfaction stems directly from our inability to understand and embrace our innermost nature.

Since Kaplinski comes from a country in which 75% of the land is under cultivation, it is hardly surprising to hear him remark, "To occupy oneself with biology and nature in practice as well as in theory is a vast and noble undertaking. This begins with the observation of nature: photographing birds, feeding animals, describing plants; and ends with a universal science of nature which transforms the world into what I have previously called Utopia, and what formerly was called the realm of peace, The Golden Age." Marx called for the humanization of nature and the naturalization of people. If, in his poems, Kaplinski calls for the "naturalization of people," it is because he knows, as our own Robinson Jeffers did, that we cannot long stand apart.

In the poetry of Jaan Kaplinski, there is not simply a beginning and an ending, nor is there justification for ends and beginnings; there is only the going itself. His poems are recordings of discoveries made along the Way. He is an anthropological ecologist, a husbandman to the human spirit. His poems bring us a sense of history and consequence. He is a poet of uncommon dignity and grace.

SAM HAMILL
April 1985
Port Townsend, Washington

PART I

NEW BUTTERFLIES ARE MADE of dust and color, but we
are planted in the ground like broken bones to replace ourselves.
Somewhere in storm and darkness, waves lap newborn islands
　　　like the lioness licks her cubs.
Words take their first steps on the darkness of white pages
　　　where there are no shadows, no depths, no distances
until something utterly new is born co-ordinate with Aurora
　　　　　　　　　　　　　　　　　　　Borealis
　　　and silver-starred hammer-blows fall through deep sleep,
walls touch fingers and sap hums in the maple's virgin heart.
Once we were to meet our children's, our parents' blood.
　　　Red strawberries stretch out their hands and geraniums are
　　　　　　　　　　　　　　　　　　strangely silent.
Dunes grow here as if white sand remembered the murmur
　　　of the rivers of paradise. Lone ants lose themselves in the
　　　　　　　　　　　　　　　　wind, carnations
blaze up on beaches, something burns unavoidably, and night
　　　　　　　　　　　　　　　　　　　sleeps
　　　in the moor's warm lap while nearby star clusters break in
　　　　　　　　　　　　　　　　　　its hair.
Fleet memory filled with ancient waterfall roars, seashells,
　　　and bees asleep behind dark walls –
will anything be reborn? Everything burns deep, deep,
　　　coals blanch and arteries harden,
and when the time comes to rise, ashes won't let go our hands,
　　　wing-feathered spring fog freezes.
How does the child's smile lose itself in the king's chamber,
　　　where does clover, that four-leafed fortune, find courage
　　　　　　　　　　　　　　　　　　to grow
　　　beneath these forbidding pillars
when even the black inscriptions on the birches fade and the
　　　　　　　　　　　　　　　　leaves' green flight
　　　wearies before clay becomes clay and the bloody mud sinks
　　　　　　　　　　　　　　　　back into soil?
No, no one anywhere needs your history, your ends and
　　　　　　　　　　　　　　　　beginnings.
Peace. Simple peace to the jellyfish, and to grouse eggs; peace,

to the ant's rushing pathways; peace, to birds of paradise
                                    and to the ginko
    peace, to the sky; peace, to you snipe's flight
peace, to apples, pears, plums, apricots, oranges,
    wild roses growing on the railroad guardshack:
Requiem, Requiem æternum.

SAILS COME SAILING OUT
from foreign pictures
sails on the Yangtze
sails on the River Li

Sun
golden fish swimming over green rocks
sky with birds
seen through falling petals

Look to the east the shadow
of a white cloud
slants over glittering water
on the horizon
emerging
white sails   sails   sails

VERCINGETORIX SAID: Cæsar, you can take
the land where we live away from us,
but you cannot take the land from us where we have died.

I've thrown down my sword at your feet.
That is how we are, my people and I;
I know what is coming.
All those who deserved to live
in the Arvernian land are dead,
and I do not want to live
with those who are left.

I know they will, I can see them
learning the tongue of the masters, forgetting their fathers'
speech.
I see them shamed by their eyes' blueness,
by their elders and their uncouth talk,
I see them as Romans clutching the papers of citizenship to their
breasts.

So be it, Imperator. Let there be one language
in your republic, one faith and one people,
let the road be secure and smooth
for your soldiers, merchants, and thieves
as far as Ultima Thule
and up to the River Styx.

I shall be flogged to death on the Capitol
but my love and my anger
cannot be put to death.
My anger will remain alive
to shout like an owl in the hollow years.
Destruction to you and to your insatiable city,
Cæsar!
Revenge will rise up like an oak
from the acorn of your desires.

Your state will come and go.
Wheat will grow on your squares, and goats will graze on your
                                                        Forum.
It is my hand and the hand of my people
that will bring you down,
my hand wielding the sword of the Vandals.

The hour will arrive when Roman pride
will not bend a single blade of grass beside the Roman road,
the hour will arrive when the gluttonous city
will burst like a leech beneath the fists of those
who come from the East and the South and the North.

Do what you want and will:
I know sword and club await me
because all who deserved to live
in the Arvernian land are dead.

Ballad of Mary's Own Land

No strength any more: Sakala weakens, Nurmekund sways,
sated ravens above us, and beneath us sooty snows.

The fortress of Rävälä rises high over the flashing flood.
The city is alien and large, and alien, too, is your blood

and Oandi and Otepää. There you stop on the billowing road.
Hammering sounds from the hilltops, orders in foreign words.

Look over the sea and the forests, watch places and names
                                                    disappear.
Look at Vaiga as long as you can while Alutaguse is still here.

One random shriek of an eagle, the flight of the one-day moth —
if you lose your songs and your language, it is total loss.

Wait a while. The lakes will vanish; from the sea, the coast will
                                                              rise,
salt sea water will eat out your heart and rust away your eyes;

sunk to the salty bottom, you sleep under crumbling ice.
The engines of siege are dragged to Saarde over your sunken
                                                            face.

OUR SHADOWS are very long
when we return at night from haying
but we ourselves are small

The camomile clasps its hands together
as if in prayer
A woman with a sickle creeps up the hill
as she did a thousand years ago

Beyond the courtyard
the heath
beyond the heath forest

Heather heather-colored
whither dost thou fly little bee
that heaven
is so vast and void
once we will return
once we will all return.

ONLY TO GO ALONG, only to go along,
always there is spring somewhere,
there is rain somewhere.

Only to go along, only to go hand in hand with spring
where there was a desert yesterday, where he who goes
was himself a desert yesterday, full of mirages and memories
where red and yellow poppies like armies
rise from the dead;
only to go and see with one's own eyes there's no need to stay,
no need to finish anything before going on, no need to guard
                                                        the grave
on this morning of the resurrection of the yellow poppies.

Only to go along, no need to take a thing,
no need to return, no need to return from that
third morning of desert flowers
to oneself, to one's headache, angina pectoris, white bedsheets,
the place of one's grave:
only to see, only to be with him,
to be with poppies, cacti, amaryllises, mesembryanthemums.

Let him who believes in duty fold the sheets,
let someone advertise a free gravesite in the papers.
One who was sick, one who had been buried, was lost without
                                                        a trace
on the third day.

Two days ago, the thunderbird broke its shell
and they all heard it: lilies, amaryllises, poppies, the hedgehog
                                                heads of cacti,
and the mesembryanthemums in their stony sleep.
Yesterday the grass burned on the savannah, the dry blades of
                                                        grass,

and today they are all here, only you have to come to see –
only to come and look, catch him and follow him,
follow the spring that walks somewhere over the listening earth:
he is always somewhere, he is always everywhere.

YOU, YOU MOON – in whose laps did you place darkness
    before there was night?
Do you remember, the day stood before the new pages
    and didn't dare come in.
March waited at the head of the bed blowing her fists,
    April emerged from the sea-foam.
Everything else was just the wind whistling,
    burnt books flying overhead.
Do you remember the resurrection, have you forgotten the life?
    After all, you know where we were buried. Put
    your ear to the ground and listen:
a train faraway? No! No armor, no pneumatic hammer, no –
    air rustling in the pits of lungs, pulse beating.
The light brings back the white butterfly from beyond Pluto's
                                       orbit.

WHITE CLOVER ASKS NOTHING
but when they ask in whose name
I will reply in the name of white clover

only bones and tin buckles remain after soldiers
resin has eaten the crosses from the pines
white white white clover

one stalk three leaves: Father Son Holy Spirit
dark needles bark fluttering in the wind
crimson was the question green is the answer

IN EVERY EYE
of every globe-flower
last year's sun rises
and silently watches
with its own eyes

remembering nothing
the curlews are jubilant

WHO HAS WHO HAS EVER
rowed across the river
to other shore
is always
across the river

here and there
the same yellow buttercups
are burning into ashes

SUMMER YOU POOR SUMMER – in glittering
gossamers gray and pale
meadows potato-fields but NO
but NO let the steel lose hope let the copper tire
bells become silent and apples in the tree grow pale
I will cut new labyrinths in the yellow stone
new forests and animals and a new daylight
swallows being born and growing in the womb of sandstone cliffs
brown wings flashing over Ahja the river of my ancestors
forever forever

O DISTANT SUN
faceless nameless
silvering light
flashing on fish
lake blooming its blooming
bird
calls to bird
from dusk to dawn
sleeping rustling rushes

———————

words only words
empty vessels in empty space
everything else
is one and the same – a world
which never was
and never will be

nobody is and cannot
be anything – what
does this solitude mean

———————

Blue – too blue
high swing above the shore
strange sun and wind

ants
scattered over bare sand
carnations rise from the earth
the land
belongs to us to me to no one

IF YOU WANT TO GO
do not remain if only for our sake
because we do not understand – thirty years
forty years of thirst of sunsets and sunrises in dusty windows
who then can say to us whither and how long yet
who then will answer us if you
take your hand
from your mother's hand
from your father's hand
and the wind takes your hand and you go

on aspen leaves
the tiny feet of the sun walk
into evening
today always and for a long time yet

we are given too much and we are
very poor
we are taught too much and we know
nothing

but we too we do not want
to inhabit the same world
as an Oliver Cromwell or a Jossif Stalin

but we must remain – wagons
athwart, sideways on the road
we have no speech and no voice if you go
look back once more wait

fields are fanning green scarves
meadows are fanning motley scarves
you are melting away between grass and bumblebees

the road rises and descends again
you go and will not return – the hands of a windmill

are waving when you are already on the other side of the hill
when we all are we all will be

     everyday life hair grows even after death
     free time motorcycles cathalepsy
     paraplegy anabiosis crimes and punishments

we shall all be free we shall see
what it really is it will anyway have an end
and we have enough time do not go before us wait
some time some mile on the king's dismal plain
in the land of burnt tanks and turning wheels
because we must find the way

     long sandy straight openings
     to put your head on the naked knees of the forest
     and sleep until the end

when you forget us and smile to the windmill on the hillside
and go away who will help us
to the gate and say to them there
that we are back

     white rivers are lost in white sand
     yellow rivers are lost in yellow sand
     in the blue eyes of my child
     the land beyond forests shines

home shelter courtyard well
rooster's crow opening buds
all awake with all all together with all

     but nothing is ready yet
     nothing will ever be ready
     in the long dreams of the children
     is God Himself dreaming of His dreams

the windmill is playing with wind the road rises and descends
                                                            again
do not go yet remain
remain with us for we do not yet know a thing

    a red cloud cuts the sun into halves
    the sky is full of marlets

EVERY DYING MAN
is a child:
in trenches, in bed, on a throne, at a loom,
we are tiny and helpless
when black velvet bows our eyes
and the letters slide from the pages.
Earth lets nobody loose: it all
has to be given back – breath, eyes, memory.
We are children when the earth
turns with us through the night toward morning
where there are no voices, no ears, no light, no door,
only darkness and movement
in the soil and its thousands
of mouths, chins, jaws, and limbs
dividing everything so that   '
no names and no thoughts remain
in the one who is silent lying in the dark
on his right side, head upon knees.
Beside him, his spear, his knife
and his bracelet, and a broken pot.

I UNDERSTOOD. I understood
"the beautiful" is an illusion, it is time for æsthetics
to die. The moon sets and categories lose
their meanings. Something new
grows through the walls of Sparta.
JERICHO
blow your horn, John Coltrane blow, don't be dead,
return to be a revenant, an apparition, just don't
be silent; shriek, Ray Charles, don't forgive, Archie Shepp, blow
blow away the solid cities, the memorial tablets, the holy
                                                    scriptures,
the national heroes, classical literature, the renaissance, epics,
romantics, Young Germans, Slavophiles, Cromwell and
                                                    Richelieu,
James Cook, Columbus, Vasco da Gama, Philip, Louis, all of
                                                    them!
Blow away their discoveries and their borders, blow away
their names, their rooms and streets, away, blow away Ludwig
van Beethoven, G. W. F. Hegel Goethe Disraeli Alexander by
                                                    the grace
of God Johann Strauss Baudelaire James Joyce, away into the
                                                    winds
of oblivion, into the hot holy black winds of oblivion,
their philosophy, their music, their pride and history,
blow their banners inside out, their moneybags, genealogies,
memoirs, museums, monuments of art, tapestries, draperies,
capitals, parliaments, parties, blow away their culture,
their armless marble statues, away, back into the earth,
                                                    pantheons, Phidias
Praxiteles, broken pale statues which profaned for centuries
the free living earth, reviled the children and the sparrows
from their places on high, blow them to burning! And what is
                                                    hope –
black coal in the hard hands of rock-layers, seeds
in the black womb of earth. The color of hope is black. This is
                                                    hope:

what survived history, Augustus Columbus Vasco da Gama,
passage from the Slave Coast to the shores of the New World,
                                                    hope
is what helped the living flesh believe, to conquer chains and
                                              Calvinism,
hope is a song, the rhythm, the knocking waves breaking, the
                                         testament of
the drowned, the screams of ashes, the revenge of the Indians,
                                      the living flame,
the drummer's fists always without the past, always forever
                                              living

SANCTUS SANCTUS SANCTUS

PART II

EVERYTHING IS INSIDE OUT, everything is different —
colorless, nameless, voiceless —
the sky overhead is an axe-blade. No one knows
that what mirrors the stars and the Milky Way is an axe.
Only those who love see, and remain silent
while in the sky the mirror-blade gets loose and falls
through us, a black starry dark
falling through a blacker dark, and nothing can stop it.
It falls no matter how we turn, always,
it hits us and divides head from body.
The sound of the abyss rises like clouds through us.
Twin stars are overhead: one light, one dark.
Everything else is illimitable void and distant,
dust motes whirling through a dark cathedral, everything else
is a black shawl where the fine old fire has written our names too.

SLEEP COVERS US too much for one, too little for two.
Your toes are naked in defiance of the winter night.
Red foxes move like flames in the mountains.
Pentatonics: your little finger *is* little,
and on your closed eyelids the middle and elder brothers
slide back into the fairy tale.

But some day much later, I will recall the shore,
awakening beside you after death in a dream.
There are broken trees and splinters of ships
and crosses for the departed who, perhaps, have arrived.
Once, the sheet will glide from us. Once, the eyes will stiffen
and a common grave will hold the brothers. If then, too,
if then too, what then? Why? What, my love?

NON-BEING PERVADES EVERYTHING and being is full of peace.
Your translation of Lao-tse can be right or wrong – an open
                                                         book
speaks today as an open butterfly and in the pollen
movement meets immobility in the same way.
The spring breeze flows through our hair and clothes.
If I speak, it is because the consolation is so much more
than ourselves waiting for it: waters breaking in from
                                                everywhere,
the tent-roof taking flight in the clear night of Lappland,
necklaces falling shattered: phrases, life and wisdom.
So this is it, this is you. The eyes are melting
in the white clouds, it is love, love that cuts us
from squared paper and lets the fire warm us
and the rain come through us until between the earth and us
the last borderlines vanish. This is love: the leaves of trees
and the light like ourselves full of evidence of the infinite.
We shall be and we shall be what is not,
we shall remain what belongs to no one.

THEY ARE STANDINNG up to their knees in blood and mud,
up to their knees, *not on their knees,*
at the gas chambers, *not gas stoves,*
saying that life is beautiful...
I cannot, I cannot once more...

The world is a dark surface,
a polished surface aslant, aslant,
a world aslant toward Auschwitz,
aslant my town,
my town, my home, my wife and child
high up on the thin edge – below,
only smooth polished wood,
black wood, and high up
you, me, all of us
and looking down one feels
his heart falling, his blood flowing straight down,
down – *no one is strong enough,*
nobody demolished the gas chambers,
nobody made peace:
this all exists from the beginning,
war in peace, peace in war. All in all,
how long can we stand here, how long
believing life is beautiful,
that *everyone gets his due,* that *work makes us free?*
Under millions of eyes that are ashes
we are standing on a sleek thin board
above millions of eyes that are ashes.

Only together with them might one be happy,
and they are looking at me with millions of eyes
and my pale blood is flowing straight down
hoping to find a pure hope, a handful of pure land
under the sun's distorting mirror, under this slanting land,
these white clouds and the jubilant endless indifference
of the last skylarks.
My love, I am again falling on my eyes

into the ashes of those I could have been,
on my eyes into their burnt eyes
as if it were not painful enough to be born
on white sheets under a dark light
to become executioner or victim. I know
that everything is
only lightning reflected in dewdrops, suffering
the more distant, the more real, what was forgotten
returns in this way, towers breaking, railways melting,
fishes drowning – my eyes, why
do you not help me – dead,
why do you not help me to live – the Creator
has not yet said his first word? But
has the end not ended, the beginning not begun?
Everything is something else *for him*
who writes and reads, but no one of us
speaks truth when he says he knows why,
whither, with what, to whom, how long
we are said, written, shaped
to have a meaning. – Even that
is too much for words. PEACE
is too big. In peace
there is room for everything. But how
can I be there together with those that are not,
how can killers be together with the killed
meaning one and the same thing. TOO MUCH
you are to me, world, why
didn't you leave me in your unconscious
flowering clover?

IF I WANTED TO GO BACK
I should know that the thoughts
I thought going through the empty houses
are as empty as the houses
where moths gnaw and fungus eats
the walls and where the spinning wheel stands alone
in the corner, where the spade stands alone
before the threshold. This emptiness is great indeed,
as is the land. Each one is someone else
from everywhere and leads the way
somewhere else, and no one could ever
walk through all this land:
every beginning is different after its end
than it was before it ended, and everything is always
something else: the houses remain empty
and I haven't the strength, nobody has the strength
to live and die with everyone,
to step across your thresholds, sleep in all your beds.
My abandoned land, lifeless land, how
I try to tear myself away from you, how
can I be and live with all these new things
that have no known face or manner? Thus, I put
my hand against the moth-eaten beam
and get up, and go: the darkness lies equally on everything and
everyone,
the darkness is large enough for our land and for all of us.

ONCE MORE SPRING PULLS young leaves from buds
 and the earth hides its tears under primrose.
But a man is only a ship anchored in himself, in his history,
 his time, a big ship decaying on the village pond
forgetting there are other beings, other societies and worlds:
fishes building nests or surfacing to breathe,
 caravans of penguins arriving on the shore,
ants walking their ancient trails – the soil is alive and moves
 its endless feet, flagella, mouth, appendages and antennæ.
But a man should be clear, a mirror reflecting everything:
 this spring, these birds returning, these triangles, open
 and closed sets, and hierarchies –
a man is curved, a closed surface reflecting only himself,
 the ancient darkness in his vaults
where even candlelights are weary and names written with soot
 cover one another. Everyone wants to perpetuate himself,
 one conquers, one discovers, one wins: all looking for
themselves, for their sooty names, suitable place
 on the walls and under the vaults of history.
The darkness is deep. And cold carbonic acid gas is rising
 and white eyeless fishes are stirring in their pools,
niches in sandstone, everywhere mummies and pyramids of
                                                    bones,
 too little space for the living.
Small indeed is the consolation from what once was said
 by another buried alive, small consolation from churches
 and castles, from painting and classical music.
A man finds himself moved far away from the living:
 beside him, above him, beneath him.
He is closed in himself and has invented his own reflection
 and the reflection of that reflection: culture, literature,
 architecture. But even this is hopelessly, hopelessly little.
But then? But then, as from another space, from a world
 from under other suns, the language of the bees, the
                                           intelligence

of dolphins, a little understanding, satori, some open space
in the catacombs of our minds. A little consolation
in the oxygen deficiency.
Some wind in the gray lobes in the sclerotic vessels see
something bursting like a spring in the *fossa sylvii*
hippocampus the little sea horse skipping in its paradise of
algae
before the windows are locked with bars and the city escapes
into its soot and noise. My leaves are too white,
too futile to compare with the green, a petty testimony
compared to the sparrow's song, a testimony of the truth
that eyes are proof of seeing, ears are proof of hearing,
and no alphabet, no code, no axiom. Never. And nowhere.

LIGHT
reminds us
of something
through
the roof of
the old barn
even
when the young
grass is
already grown
through the wings

ant-path
on the eyes
your ashes
our ashes
wandering
with the rains
of centuries:
irrevocably
bound

OVEN
alone
in the corner

grandmother
alone
in the graveyard

the same
big gray
handmill:

the wind
of May
rolls
over us

WHAT WOKE US
was indeed nothing
but a dancing pea
in a turning cathedral

a little turning
girl blowing
dandelion-paratroopers
into every wind

and walls looking
toward her through
walls and the voice
returns to the beginning

NIGHT AND EARTH
breathing in the warmth
of the past day

as yours is only
what will not
be left to you

a day a thought a life
handful of foam
trembling on the sand
in wind into wind

under the seventh lock
a bird's voice
is singing
of something else

but no key
to it
in any
human tongue

wind
lick clean
stones and
our eyes
with your warm
moist
salty tongue

To be
Icarus
and fall
wings aflame
into
the burning
buttercups
which

recapture
your own
nameless
fatherland

some passage
some island
some utopia

gets
your name

HONEYBEES
through
sunshine

rising
dancing
falling
dust:

a moment of
being
so full
of joy

even
without
any wish
that everyone
read
from your glance
the end
of the poem

YOU
LIGHT-FOOTED MOSS
already
on
the window frame
already
on the roof

to walk
on tiny
feet
which
arrived
so long
before you

on fingers
which
guarded you
in the almost
intolerable
world

long
before
you knew
how
to see
them
and
name them

Near
nearest
distant

they all
become this
same yellow
voiceless
chicken
in the courtyard of
another death
et cetera

thin
sharp thread
which ties
your heart
with one and
the same
relentless
sorrow
of them all

trembling edge-
wise the shadow
of an aspen
leaf through
your eyes
into you

like a platinum
thread
to weigh
stars

constellations
but never
never
your own
heart

THE SAME
SEA
in us all
red
dark
warm

throbbing
winds from
every quarter
in the sails
of the heart

line
of foam through
white
space

question falling
from the oar
rolling
back
on the wave
fear
behind the darkness

or the same
sea
waiting
for another

BIG BLACK HEDGEHOG
eternity descending
into the valley

a spiny ball
melting
in the hands
of a child

all
frontiers
barbed wire
of
the world

walking
like hedgehogs
over
all frontiers

children's eyes
resting
like butterflies
at
your feet

A FLYING FISH
takes wing
from the book

through the seal
of the Milky Way
on the swell

on the other
side where
the great sea
dissolves
everything
to its primeval
elements

even
death
too little
for this
great
world

ANT TRAIL
on a
poplar's
gnarled
trunk

memory
small light
in the damp
cloud

then
between
two worlds
you lose
direction

what pulls
you upward
is it
your weight

what pulls
you down
is it
your wings

not yet grown
yet growing

SUMMER'S
LAST EVENING
cloudy
and warm

no one
you visited
was at home

two useless
bottles
of wine
in your bag

everyone
you met
in the street
was drunk

everybody
drunk
in the street

SO LIGHT
after all
this great and
evil world
built
of butterflies'
wings

springtimes
big cities
pestilences
gliding
over history

you
me
who does
need
consolation

fluttering
of motley
wings

caught
by a gust
over
the lake

you too
long ago
cast
your last
glance

said
your last
word

HEART
OF RAIN
where nothing
stirs

only the
difference
of black
and white
halving
a random
falling
drop

Nymphalis Io
wings
folded on
the smithy
window

poems
and flames
dying out
in the great
joy
of waters
that meet

in the little
flowing
world
the tears
lose
meaning

ASHES
of one world
crumble
upon the colors
of another one

the sunflower
lost
its crown

hoarfrost
on the scythe
grasshoppers
silent

three sheep
in the fog
the rowan tree
stripped
of leaves
and berries

to write
write
something
something
else

PAINTING
a boat
you need not
paint the water

painting
a smile
you need not
paint the face

painting
a blossom
you need not
paint the flower

and you can say
you have to bear
a mote
from the immense
weightlessness
of the world.

THE LATE WELL-MASTER
of Veskimoisa
lives on
unlike the others

In water
in springs

From under
the lid
thrust aside
from the dark square
his sky looks
every day
into your eyes

Is the mud
always
the last
to step
back
into its tracks

you asked
once

and the answer
flows
into you
as air
as sand
as night.

WITH A BROKEN WING
somebody whisks off
the letters
and breadcrumbs

children are picking up
motley pens
in the courtyard

perhaps it is better
if no one thinks
which were the wings
that bore me once

high above
this strange earth

as snow
as ash
as water

I will come I will flow back
little by little
to everywhere

and when someone
standing on
the roadside will count
kernels from an ear
in his hand or
gather his pockets
full of acorns

no one of them
will ever recognize
me again

EVERYTHING MELTS
burns out:
lamp lamp-shade
the light itself
with no shade left

no world
belongs to you and you
belong
to no world

you are pulled
by rain and light
on roads coming
and going
from everywhere
to everywhere

THE HOUSE silent
water drippings
from a rinsed diaper
into the empty basin
everybody already asleep

I forgot
a short poem that
came into my mind
sitting in the rocking chair
with my little daughter
in my lap

I did not dare
to take a pencil
and write it down
feeling this silence
and the sleeping child
has a meaning
deeper than words

A TITMOUSE
upside down
picking last seeds
from a frost-bitten sunflower

we came back
bees had abandoned their hives
a dead mouse
was floating in the well

north wind roaming
over dead grass
in our garden
and hillside

at night
we stood long
on the stairs
with the boys
and looked for
Taurus and Aries
rising from the southeast
a rat was hustling
through dead vines

this fall
space for a while
more real than time

INK not yet
dried
loaf of bread
not yet
eaten

spring
come
and gone

colors
growing
again and
again on
my burnt
happy
wings

which do not
know if they
belong to
a philosopher
or
to a butterfly

WIPING AWAY
dust
washing away
mud
from the ten
boots
of my family

waiting for snow

time goes
winter goes

THE WAY TURNS toward the heath
dead windmills stand
against darkness
in the whole world
there is nothing
but the scent of red clover
and nothing more

SWARMS OF DAWS
are flying
home
from the west

black
on the purple background
of the sunset

over the town
depot
over hundreds
of elbowing people
gray in the dusk

who do not know
what to do
with their large
black wings

going home
going to work

SOUL'S RETURNING

Actually, there is much more than sadness and joy —
that growing and ebbing of light in the forest and orchard
even in the apple grove, yours and your children's homeground,
                                                something
immediate which time before death can't make familiar

and this bird, but this bird, how else can I name
who I listen for through this icy darkness

what, who moves behind the glass moves me, reaches into me,
through me, is gone yet exists, so that I am and live
and despair and sing and

though I know this is not really true, it is simply good
to be shadow, to be a tiny tongue of flame in this huge blind
wind

how can one
keep forgetting
those other
lands
and rivers
from whence
to where

although

I too
have been there

although

they have
been in me

although

I don't know
whether in front
or behind
or around
or inside
the importance
rests in reconciling
with the people
of those lands
if there
are
any

is there really
any limit
between
oneself
and something
or somebody
do I stand
in the sluice-gate
or in the furnace
do I
flow
or burn

flame
fire —
or water —
fall murmuring
shuddering
all around

scorched birds
in some other
sky
singing an unfinished
song
drowned fish
laughing
over
fishermen's
bones
of the joy
that erases
love
and anger

furnace mouth
sluice-gate
high up
down deep
all
is burned
flowed
forgotten

hillocks
like stones
like grain
tumbled
into valleys
clover straightened
in footprints

just one
cricket
saws
on this and that
threshold of hearing

behind the window
melting snow
forms
strange
round drops

so long
you were
away
so long
coming
back
we see something, but it isn't light that we see
because we don't see light, all things, all of us
are fragments of that which I can only name
light – although I know there is no darkness it can't
reach – but from our side light
slivers appear as darkness around us which separates us
from everything, even from ourselves
words form their meaning and there is no answer
to why something real becomes unreal
only words, lying empty words, old sayings, pronouns
adjectives, exclamations swirl around us and if
something connects us, then it is the wind from their wings
and that words reach the unseen, we may
read more into words than they contain or that we contain,
                                                    words
are the first to cut through gray cataracts, words sometimes
take flight, and are away, call for us to follow but we
don't come to look for the opening which is not yet closed and
                                                    when
we see what it is below and above we bounce back, grasp at any
church tower, exclamation, straw, spider web to not keep
falling into that empty roaring sea of flowers, the wave suddenly
too close, then it all fades and words return tired and
compliant, in a poem or as memory, as notes on a scale

as swallows onto a wire, once seen once felt
distance remains humming as the outstretched hand of our
deep emotion's helpless gesture to accompany us to the end

empty foolish beloved words who always cover my wounds
with your silent speckled feathers, o light, light
have you spoken to me with my own tiny whispers

earth cares
equally
for every
flying
stone and
bird

life-giver life-taker earth our anchor stone our
grave stone, big old lone stone in the dark,
emptiness – who are you – I want to ask you something
but I don't know what, I don't know yet but soon
it will be late
something
glowing
red
in white
flame
heart
in people
in snow
which all
expires
gravecandle
melting itself
a cave
in snow
the world
is all
ashes

dead
flames' hearth
and
a glowing
dying
in the center
deep down
everything
that anyone
has ever
been
has been
fire

PART III

ALL IN ONE
one in all
mind in body
body in mind
the strange in the ordinary
the ordinary in the strange
a swarm of bees
in an old chest
in the loft
of an abandoned
farmhouse

MAY YOU BE
the mild soft
summer night
of my non-existent
childhood
covering me
with its huge
voiceless wings

EVERY UNDERSTANDING
comes in due time
your little hands
on my rough cheeks
first snow
always
to someone
for the first
for someone
for the last
time

IF I MUST BE
at all then let
me be a tiny
fleeting
transparent
almost bodiless
mindless
nothing through
which can flow
the infinite
light of being
of becoming
Amitabha

INFINITE LIGHT
of the night where
the flowing world
becomes fleetingly transparent
and on my right
your breathing

we have been
so thirsty
so silent
we two together
on the seashore sometimes
in Saaremaa

THE WHITE VASE
on the white piano
glowing
through the blue
stream of dusk
that carries
me with
myself
with this house
this room
this you

I am ready
to go
to flow
it is good
like remembering
that I
have stored the matches
and firewood
for winter

A PURE AND BURNING
thirst for you
the greatest
deepest longing
gives your hand
into mine
between your two phrases
between two glances
the wind
rustles over the forest

LITTLE BY LITTLE
OUR DIRTY RIVER
flows itself clean
little by little
perhaps we too

manage
to take each other
by hand
back to the endless
purity of
this world
understanding
we have never
really left it

TODAY
forever
let me look
with your
gentle glance
through myself
through the twilight
that floods
our room
our world

LITTLE BY LITTLE
a poem fades
I dreamt
a poem about
a beautiful girl
on white sand
on the far side
of flashing water

it was written
and read
by someone else
and the longing
to flow like sand
over her legs
belonged to someone else

yours
was only
that dream you could not
be rid of

JOY
silent joy
over this silence
upon which
every instant
draws something pure
stopping my face
in both your eyes
stopping
everything
for an instant

AN UNDERSTANDING
of someone
coming nearer
from far off

everywhere
you are
only simply HERE

a pine tree in sea-wind
gray beard of lichen
swinging together
with the twig

WORDS THOUGHTS
curtains
in front of what
they ought to mean
explanations
justifications
philosophies
synthetic
washing powder
to each his own
escape in philosophy
escape from philosophy
path
back
into silence
into purity
home

I AM BOTH
spider and fly
snared in my own
web who sometimes
in the evening
thinks
how to reel
into a single ball
all these endless
sticky soul-threads
to throw them
into the blue fire
that sometimes
rises
from the bottom
of my mind
between sleep
and waking

DANA PARAMITA
from this
red fragrant strawberry
I brought you
in the evening dusk
coming home after mowing
there remained only
a gentle red glow
we see
we remember
between sleep
and waking
between
two dreams

TIME SPACE GARDEN
forest tracks
so full so full
of your absence
a strange dolorous
silence everywhere
waiting for you

THERE IS NOTHING
between us
but oblivion

something coming into mind
in your eyes
in your helpless
little hands

I have never existed
never at all

A SPRING
under alders
amid the echoless
world of twilight
reflecting
the continuous limitless
imperceptible
turning of light
into darkness

To wake
in the dead of night
from sleep
from myself
as I am
as I was
before I was born
no light no darkness
only astonishment
that I am here
and inability
to tell
how it all
really is

before and beyond
the sword-blow
of the great oblivion
that gave you
this time
and space
and name

Notes on the Poems

Vercingetorix said: Vercingetorix was the son of a Gallic tribal chief of the Averni. Following the rebellion he led against Cæsar in 52 B.C., he was executed. (See also George Seferis's poem "Fine Autumn Morning" in the *Collected Poems*.)

Ballad of Mary's Own Land: These are all place-names.

Ink: See the well-known story of Chuang Tzu and the butterfly in *Chuang Tzu* translated by Burton Watson.

If I must be: the reference is to Amitabha Buddha.

Dana paramita: (Sanscrit) the perfection of charity.

A Note on the Translation

THE POEMS of Jaan Kaplinski were first brought to my attention by my friend, Mall Peek, an American with familial roots in Estonia. Jaan Kaplinski, she told me, was the first poet ever to deeply move her. And since he had become almost the national poet of her homeland, she was searching for a collaborator to assist in producing a selection of his poems for a North American audience. She had made literal translations of four or five of his poems to show me what he was like. Reading what I now recognize as literal trots, I felt I had suddenly come into contact with a deep kindred spirit.

There were biographical connections between us, I felt: while Kaplinski is a year older, he lost his father about the same time I was orphaned; he had come under the influence of Oriental philosophy at about the same time I had turned to Rinzai Buddhism and ventured to Japan. There were also some striking differences: I had no stronger memory of World War Two than of being fed a seemingly perpetual diet of oatmeal as a result of rationing and/or poverty in the home where I was kept – hardly a correspondence with the devastation which was inflicted upon Estonia – and I was raised in one of the most powerful nations in the world, a nation of abundance. I recognized in his poems a teacher, words from a man without literary ambition, but with an enormous sense of responsibility.

But more than that, I felt a brotherly love and reverence for his poems not unlike that which I had long felt for my elders, Denise Levertov and Kenneth Rexroth, poets I had read closely all my adult life. Mall Peek and I collaborated on "finishing" her versions, and I sent them to the poet. Much to my surprise, his reply included several literal translations of his poems with a request that I continue to serve as collaborator.

During our correspondence, I discovered other connections with my distant brother: his studies of Levi-Strauss and Radin leading to conclusions not dissimilar to my own view of the value of the primitive in its most literal (primal) sense.

We completed the project with Kaplinski providing the first draft in English. I then worked from his literals, often with the aid of listening to his readings of the poems in the original Estonian, searching for basic rimes of rhythm, sensibility, and syntax. In some few cases we have chosen to add punctuation (the originals are unpunctuated) for the sake of clarity. I also benefited from referring to translations made by Ilse Lehiste, Ivar Ivask, and Ants Ert, and offer them my gratitude and admiration.

In truth, this book belongs to Mall Peek and Jaan Kaplinski. I have acted the part of midwife, more editor than translator. I am grateful. Nine bows.

Sam Hamill

Also available in Harvill Paperbacks

ANNA AKHMATOVA
Selected Poems
Translated from the Russian by
Stanley Kunitz with Max Hayward

"She displays all the emotional subtlety
of nineteenth-century Russian prose and all
the dignity that the poetry
of the same century taught her"
JOSEPH BRODSKY

HOMER
The Odyssey
Translated from the Greek by Robert Fitzgerald

"Fitzgerald is taking his place beside Chapman and Pope in the
unbroken lineage of English Homeric translations . . .
it has the economy and the soar of a poet"
GEORGE STEINER

MICHAEL O'NEILL
The Stripped Bed

"Once or twice in a decade an original talent emerges . . .
Michael O'Neill is one such . . . *The Stripped Bed* shows
more than promise; it announces a future"
ALAN ROSS

BORIS PASTERNAK
Poems 1955–1959
with
An Essay in Autobiography
Translated from the Russian by
Michael Harari and Manya Harari
Introduction by Craig Raine

"As refreshing as a stream of icy water"
STEPHEN SPENDER